# CONTENTS

# Introduction

Hill-Stead has been a hub of activity since the Pope family first occupied their newly built country estate in Farmington, Connecticut. Here, from 1901-1946, in succession, Alfred and Ada Pope and their daughter Theodate, with her career-diplomat husband John Wallace Riddle, entertained many illustrious individuals—authors, artists, poets, academics and presidents. The Popes and Riddles also extended their hospitality to town folk and employed dozens of workers, among them Earnest Bohlen, butler to the family for nearly 60 years. Today Hill-Stead is a 152-acre, nine-building museum and a National Historic Landmark. Visitors of all ages enjoy tours, programs and outdoor fun. They also find Hill-Stead an enchanting respite from their busy lives.

Hill-Stead's story begins with founder Theodate Pope Riddle, an only child of privilege, who yearned for her own dairy farm in an era when women of her class were expected to focus on family and social prominence. Ever independent, she left her hometown of Cleveland, Ohio, and continued her education in the 1880s at Miss Porter's School in Farmington. From an early age, she envisaged a future of caring for orphan children, engaging with ideas, proselytizing tasteful refinements and involving herself with community.

Self-taught as an architect, Theodate cut her professional teeth in the 1890s with the restoration of an 18th-century clapboard house and the design of Hill-Stead. Over the years she pursued various commissions and projects, with Avon Old Farms School consuming her considerable talent and resources for two decades.

This guidebook provides an overview of Hill-Stead's story and collections, including Alfred Pope's outstanding French Impressionist paintings. It is the compilation of research and writing undertaken by a team of highly qualified staff members and volunteers: Melanie Bourbeau, Cynthia Cormier, Christina Gerber, Polly Huntington, Alison Meyers, Elizabeth Normen, Brie Quinby and Sandra Wheeler. Talented Cheryl Dauphin, designer, laid out the book and helped bring our vision to fruition. I especially want to express heartfelt thanks to the donors who generously supported this publication: the State of Connecticut, Department of Economic and Community Development, The Henry L. and Grace Doherty Charitable Foundation, Robert and Beth von Dohlen, Mark and Tracey Lunenburg, and Charles P. Reagan.

It is my great pleasure to welcome you to Hill-Stead.    ⌂


Linda M. Steigleder
Director

I closed my eyes and thought, "this is of course the end of life for me," and then I thought of you, dearest mother, and knew Gordon [foster child] would be of comfort to you.  I was glad I had made another will, and counted the buildings I had designed—the ones built and building, and hoped I had "made good."

—THEODATE POPE TO HER MOTHER IN SUMMER 1915, JUST WEEKS
  AFTER HER EXPERIENCE ON THE SINKING OF THE R.M.S. LUSITANIA

# Theodate Pope Riddle, Architect

*Salem, Ohio, February 2, 1867 –*
*Farmington, Connecticut, August 30, 1946*

Theodate Pope Riddle designed Hill-Stead as a traditional farmhouse, but here the classic wood frame
structure is writ large. Completed in 1901 as the
crown jewel of a 250-acre property, the 33,000-
square-foot house with attached theater stands
today as one of America's most important examples
of Colonial Revival domestic architecture. The
façade of the house, modeled after America's most
prominent Colonial house, George Washington's
Mount Vernon, makes for an impressive statement
as visitors arrive by way of Hill-Stead's tree-lined
drive. Though this grand house was fully outfitted

*Theodate Pope
Riddle,* c. 1921

Harris Ewing,
Washington, D.C.,
Photographer

Archives,
Hill-Stead Museum

for entertaining and the comfort of guests, outwardly it was
meant to signal our nation's history, particularly its New
England traditions. Louvered shutters or blinds, clapboard
siding, and simple yet classic architectural details, together
with the adjoining outbuildings, mimic farmsteads of the
1700s. Theodate's goal in creating this new home was to make
it look as if it had been *in situ* for generations.

Theodate was in her 20s when she sidestepped society's expec-
tations and trained to become an architect. She apprenticed
on the job and pursued private tutorials with Princeton
University professors at a time when few women matriculat-
ed in architecture schools. Her work at Hill-Stead is the product of an unusual partnership. Lacking technical skills,
Theodate tapped the prestigious New York architecture firm
of McKim, Mead & White for assistance and architectural
drawings. Theodate's clients were her parents, Alfred Atmore
and Ada Brooks Pope. The Gilded Age industrialist and his
wife wanted interiors suitable for showcasing their excep-

*Theodate Pope visits Mt. Vernon, c. 1900*

Archives, Hill-Stead Museum

tional collection of French Impressionist paintings and other art-work and furnishings. Then and now, four Claude Monet paintings hang in Hill-Stead's interiors along with masterpieces by Édouard Manet, Edgar Hillaire Degas, Mary Cassatt and James McNeill Whistler.

Theodate's success with Hill-Stead lies in her melding of two opposing forms—the New England farmhouse with the opulent grand-scale country house. Hill-Stead epitomizes the Colonial Revival style, a phenomenon that gained popularity in the United States with the 1876 Centennial celebration and continued through the 1930s (and arguably is still with us today). This decades-long movement developed in reaction to rapid industrialization, urbanization and large-scale immigration. It was a nostalgic assertion that America's Colonial roots represent the "true" America.

## Birth of an Architect

Theodate thrived in a field dominated by men. Yet if her father's life exemplified the Gilded Age, then his daughter's was both a product of and reaction to it. In a time when women could not vote, Theodate insisted on playing by her own rules, though always with the safety net of her father's wealth. In her hometown of Cleveland, Ohio, she attended a private girls school along with the daughters of Presidents Garfield and Hayes. At 19, Theodate continued her education at Miss Porter's School from 1886 to 1888. The charming Village of Farmington, Connecticut, with housing that dates back to the 1700s, captured her imagination.

After finishing at Miss Porter's School, Theodate embarked on a year-long Grand Tour with her parents. With her parents she visited museums, galleries and private collections in over 50 European cities, and learned firsthand about the Impressionists. While traveling, she agonized over and finally rejected a marriage proposal by suitor Harris Whittemore, the son of Mr. Pope's business associate. She discussed possible careers with her father and dreamed of owning and operating a small New England farm. She sketched and made notes on buildings and scenes and especially admired the beauty of the English countryside. Later, Cotswold vernacular and Tudor styles would profoundly influence her architectural designs.

*Theodate with Miss Porter's School classmates,* c. 1886

From left: unknown friend, Alice Hamilton, Theodate, Agnes Hamilton, Elizabeth Brooks (Theodate's cousin)

Archives, Hill-Stead Museum

Upon their return, Theodate made her debut into Cleveland society at the age of 21, and then with her parents' blessing settled in Farmington, eager to build a life of her own. Not far from Miss Porter's School she rented and eventually purchased an "old brown house," naming this 18th-century saltbox "The O'Rourkery." Theodate spent several years restoring the house, and thus began her practical training as an architect. She lived simply by her own well-heeled standards: "I am to have a little house in Farmington!...I am to see [to] the furnishing of it myself, bearing in mind of course that too much money must not be spent on it. I am to have a guernsey [*sic*] cow, a pig and chickens, also a garden & perhaps bees. Sara will in all probability go with me, as she can cook & will do anything for me she can."[1]

[1] Theodate Pope Diary, May 21, 1890, Archives, Hill-Stead Museum.

*Theodate Pope
with dog Silas and
cat by the Keeping
Room hearth at the
O'Rourkery,* c. 1902

Gertrude Käsebier,
Photographer

Alfred Atmore Pope
Collection, Hill-Stead
Museum

Theodate was not unique in undertaking this restoration project. During the 1890s the Colonial Revival was at its height, and throughout New England, upper-class women were saving old houses and restoring them according to a romanticized vision of Colonial life. During the 1880s and 1890s, Farmington's own Village Improvement Society worked to "clean up" the town and emphasize its Colonial heritage. Accurate historic preservation based on sound architectural and archival research would not be commonplace until decades later. Theodate, for instance, changed the exterior of The O'Rourkery from brown to a light color, probably white, even though white paint was rarely, if ever, available in Colonial times.

## Hill-Stead: A Great New House on a Hilltop

Alfred Pope wanted to own a country estate back East near family and friends. His goal coincided with Theodate's dream of establishing a New England farmstead. He purchased tracts of land on the hill behind The O'Rourkery, ultimately amassing 250 acres.[2] Theodate sited the Pope house at the crest of a hill on the newly acquired land, as if to announce the wealth and prominence of its residents. Hill-Stead was her second on-the-job architectural experience. In the fall of 1898 she wrote for assistance to the country's premier architects, McKim, Mead & White.[3] Working with Edgerton Swartout, a junior architect at the firm, Theodate absorbed technical information and involved herself in minute details, from specifications for doors and windows, to state-of-the-art heating, lighting and plumbing systems. Hill-Stead might be

[2] Today, Hill-Stead is 152 acres.
[3] McKim, Mead & White received over 1,000 commissions between 1870 and 1920, ranging from Newport mansions to the Boston Public Library and Pennsylvania Station in New York City.

a Colonial-style clapboard house with hand wrought nails, wide porches, mismatched roof lines and clustered forms, with interiors featuring ells, fireplaces, faux graining, raised panel doors, heavy brass hardware and built-ins, but Theodate ensured that it was equipped with the latest modern conveniences. She included numerous bathrooms and gas lighting for the comfort of residents and guests.

In the spring of 1901, Alfred and Ada Pope moved into their "great new house on a hilltop," as American novelist and occasional houseguest Henry James later described it.[4] But Theodate was not quite finished with her ambitious vision. In the fall of 1901 she consulted with McKim, Mead & White and added a Mount Vernonesque verandah.

From *American Homes and Gardens*, vol. VII, no. 2, February, 1910

Archives, Hill-Stead Museum

## Hill-Stead: A Significant Landscape

Hill-Stead's landscape, though altered over time by natural forces, is as integral to Theodate's design and vision as the house itself. Theodate connected her parents' country retreat and farm to the community by omitting formal entrance gates and providing bluestone walkways to the Village and Miss Porter's School. Theodate chose the site primarily for its vistas. Landscape architect Warren H. Manning, protégé of Frederick Law Olmstead and a pioneer in the nascent field of landscape architecture, advised her on the layout of the

---

[4] Luminaries who visited Hill-Stead included artist Mary Cassatt, architect Cass Gilbert, author Henry James, psychologist William James, author Sinclair Lewis, poet Archibald MacLeish, First Lady Eleanor Roosevelt, President Theodore Roosevelt, poet Edna St. Vincent Millay, journalist Ida Tarbell and author Thornton Wilder.

grounds. He called for "an American farmstead" in which "woods, fields, horizon, and…sky [did] the job." The estate appeared as though it had been extant for generations, with its mature maple and elm trees near the house and Colonial-style dry laid stonewalls. Ultimately, the estate became suc-

From *American Homes and Gardens*, vol. VII, no. 2, February 1910

Archives, Hill-Stead Museum

cessful not only as a place of beauty, but also as a place of productivity. Theodate designed and built barns and cottages, and ran her farm as a private experiment station for cattle and sheep breeding, sanitation and other progressive animal husbandry practices. Today, evidence of Hill-Stead's agricultural activity is found in the barns and outbuildings clustered near Route 4. A renovated pre-existing 18th-century farmhouse, the only building on the property not of Theodate's design, also remains.

At Hill-Stead, as in the English park, natural features determine layout: gardens, lawns and meadows flow into one another. The Sunken Garden, for instance, fits into a natural depression and is planted with perennials according to a c. 1920 planting plan by Beatrix Farrand.[5] Along the entrance drive, an allée of maple trees guides visitors and further dramatizes the

[5] Farrand was a noted landscape architect and a founding member of the American Society of Landscape Architects. Among her projects are the gardens at Dumbarton Oaks in Washington, D.C. and the Peggy Rockefeller Rose Garden at the New York Botanical Garden.

expanse of lawn surrounding the house. Beyond the house, the property opens up to include vistas of dairy barns and hay fields. Today, wooded walking paths and Theodate's "100 steps" link Hill-Stead with a region-wide trail system. Hill-Stead originally boasted a wild garden, vegetable garden, greenhouse, orchards, tennis court and golf grounds with pond.

## Theodate's Architecture Practice

Theodate established her professional architecture practice in 1905. She created her own designs and hired draftsmen to translate her ideas into working drawings. She opened her first office in New York in 1913 and maintained a field office at Hill-Stead that she called "Underledge." She was licensed as an architect in New York State and Connecticut in 1916 and 1933, respectively, and was admitted to the American Institute of Architects in 1918. One of her first projects was altering Hill-Stead, adding the Second Library and the Morning Room with its Greek Revival-style porch for her father to use as a home office. Ever the innovator, in 1917, she added the Makeshift Theater to Hill-Stead, where she showed movies on a silver screen and held parties for local children.

Theodate's first outside commission was designing Westover School, founded by her former Miss Porter's teacher and dear friend, Mary Hillard, who became the school's first head-mistress. Located in Middlebury, Connecticut, Westover is still in operation today, the brainchild of two women determined to build an ideal setting for the education of girls. At Westover, Theodate melded the mid-18th-century American Georgian style with elements of 16th-century British architecture. She also designed much of the school's furniture.

Next, Theodate designed private residences. She created a two-story house in Middlebury, Connecticut, for Columbia University law professor Joseph Chamberlain, again merging early British and American architectural styles, but with the

*Westover School, Middlebury, Connecticut,* c. 1920

Archives, Avon Old Farms School, Avon, Connecticut

British influence gaining ascendancy. The dominant feature was a steep roof with narrow dormers. Theodate carefully sited the house to take advantage of expansive views. In 1913-1914, she designed three small houses for Hill-Stead workers in Farmington and a country house for Mrs. Charles O. Gates in Locust Valley, Long Island, New York. The latter was the largest domestic construction of Theodate's career. For the Chamberlain and Gates houses, she stepped away from clapboard siding and instead used brick, stone, stucco and tile.

In 1914, Harris Whittemore, Theodate's former suitor, commissioned her to design Hop Brook School, a public elementary school in Naugatuck, Connecticut. Since then the school has been restored and enlarged, but retains Theodate's progressive design. Her most prestigious commission was the reconstruction of Theodore Roosevelt's birthplace in New York City. The Victorian boyhood home of the President had been torn down and a group of women, including the President's sister Anna Roosevelt Cowles, organized to create "a third American shrine to be visited in years to come, as

*Mrs. Charles O. Gates' House, Locust Valley, Long Island, New York,* c. 1920

Archives, Avon Old Farms School, Avon, Connecticut

Mount Vernon and the Lincoln log cabin are now visited by an ever-increasing host of patriotic pilgrims." Open to the public and operated by the National Park Service, the house was authentically recon-structed. Theodate intro-duced necessary modifica-tions to address its modern function as a museum. The companion building next door, also designed by Theo-date, houses a library, read-ing rooms, reception rooms, tea gardens and exhibition areas for the display of Roosevelt memorabilia.

*Theodate Pope and Roosevelt Association Trustees at Theodore Roosevelt Birthplace, New York, New York,* c. 1922

Archives,
Hill-Stead Museum

Avon Old Farms School in Avon, Connecticut, was Theodate's most ambitious professional project, occupying her from 1922 to 1946. In addition to designing the buildings, she helped develop the curriculum, hire staff and oversee operations. She built the school as a memorial to her parents and financed the undertaking with her inheritance. She had studied the vernacular style of the Cotswold's region and later claimed that while on a trip to England she "drew with-in a minute and a half the rough outline of all the build-ings." To ensure authentic 16th- and 17th-century tech-niques, she brought British craftsmen to Avon. At the height of construction, 500 workmen were on her payroll. Theodate insisted that "the stone and brick masons build without their plumbs or levels... [to] give freedom to the stone pattern," a manifestation of the Arts and Crafts ideology that favors a handcrafted appearance over machine-made perfection. Wherever possible, she used native materials, such as the red sandstone quarried from the site and timber from nearby woods. Metal hinges, doorknobs and lanterns were manufac-tured in the school's forge.

*Theodate Pope on site during the building of Avon Old Farms School, Avon, Connecticut, c. 1921*

Archives, Hill-Stead Museum

*Avon Old Farms School, Water Tower and Workshops under Construction, November 1923*

Edward P. Beckwith, Photographer

Archives, Hill-Stead Museum

The school opened on 2,700 acres in 1927 while construction was still underway. When the Great Depression intervened, only one of two planned quadrangles was completed and included a bank, refectory, professors' cottages, the dean's house, dormitories, carpenter shop, wheelwright shop, water tower, station house, power house, mill and forge. These buildings reflected Theodate's curriculum, which called for "the healthy interaction of farm and school by which the vitality of the soil enriches the mind, and the training of the brain is aided by the work of the hands."

## Theodate Pope Riddle: A Complex Life, An Enduring Legacy

In 1910 Theodate traveled alone to the British Isles, complete with her own car and chauffeur. During the trip, she became acquainted with novelist Henry James, whose friendship she enjoyed over many years, as evidenced in their lively correspondence. With his brother William James she investigated and supported experiments in psychical research. In May of 1915 she traveled to England to visit the British Society of Psychical Research. She was a passenger on the R.M.S. Lusitania when it was torpedoed by a German submarine; she was fortunate to be among the survivors. One year later, at age 49, Theodate married 52-year-old John Wallace Riddle, whom she had met 12 years earlier through Farmington neighbor Anna Roosevelt Cowles. In 1914 she had taken in a two-year-old orphan, Gordon Brockway, who died in 1916. In 1917 and 1918 she took in two more orphaned boys, each age 10, whom she raised as foster children. Writing to her mother in 1917, Theodate commented, "Seeing life through the eyes of [my] boys seems to comfort me more than anything."

*Theodate Pope and John Wallace Riddle on their wedding day at Hill-Stead, May 6, 1916*

Davis and Sanford, Co., Photographers

Archives, Hill-Stead Museum

During much of their marriage, Theodate and John traveled widely. In 1919 they took an extensive tour of Japan, Korea and China. Thereafter, with few exceptions, she traveled annually to Europe, and spent six months in Argentina during her husband's posting as U.S. Ambassador between 1921 and 1925. Throughout her travels, however, Hill-Stead remained Theodate's home, and architectural projects continued to be her main focus.

Theodate Pope Riddle died in 1946. Her will stipulated that Hill-Stead become a museum as a memorial to her parents and "for the benefit and enjoyment of the public." She called for the house and its collection to remain intact, not to be moved, lent or sold. Along with Hill-Stead, all of Theodate Pope Riddle's buildings stand today as enduring testimony to one of this country's earliest important women architects. ♠

# Family Biographies

*Alfred Atmore Pope, in golfing attire, relaxes on Hill-Stead's north porch, c. 1910*

Archives, Hill-Stead Museum

## Alfred Atmore Pope

*N. Vassalboro, Maine, July 4, 1842 – Farmington, Connecticut, August 5, 1913*

In 1861, when Alfred Pope was 19, he and his family moved to a Quaker community in Salem, Ohio. Later, in Cleveland, he joined his father and brothers as partners in a woolen business. Alfred married Ada Brooks in 1866, and their only child, Effie, was born one year later. (Effie later renamed herself "Theodate" after her paternal grandmother.) In 1869 Alfred borrowed $5,000 to become a principal in the Cleveland Malleable Iron Company. He transformed the company product from agricultural machinery to parts for the booming railroads. In his late 40s, self-educated and wealthy, Alfred developed a great love and enthusiasm for art. He began collecting French Impressionist paintings when he took his family on a European Grand Tour in 1888-1889. His enthusiasm developed in tandem with that of his Naugatuck, Connecticut-based business associate, J. H. Whittemore and his son Harris, who were both buying Impressionist paintings. Alfred developed his personal aesthetic and bought only artwork he "could rise to." Hill-Stead was his retirement home, designed by his daughter, and planned with his collection and tastes in mind.

> "...in business management I have held to the doing and results, rather than to the anticipations through estimates..."

—ALFRED A. POPE, DECEMBER, 1900

## Ada Brooks Pope

*Salem, Ohio, March 31, 1844 –*
*Pasadena, California, May 6, 1920*

Ada, the third of eight children, was 18 when both parents died. She and her siblings remained very close to each other all their lives, often gathering in Vermont where their parents were born. After marrying Alfred Pope in 1866, directing the Pope household became her life's work. Her skill and grace were legendary. She enjoyed living in Cleveland, Ohio, where they eventually built a Queen Anne-style house on fashionable Euclid Avenue. The family kept an apartment in New York City as well. At first Ada was less than enthusiastic about the move to Farmington. Yet, she adapted to country living, and much of what we know about daily life at Hill-Stead derives from her avid letter writing and fastidious keeping of accounts. Ada never fully recovered from Alfred's death in 1913. In her later years she found it difficult to spend long winters at Hill-Stead, and instead joined her Brooks relatives in California.

*Ada Brooks Pope with dog Jim-Jam on Hill-Stead's verandah,* c. 1910

Archives,
Hill-Stead Museum

"[Hill-Stead]...seems to be running riot while we are away.... I do not like to be kept in the dark as to my affairs at home."

—ADA POPE IN A LETTER TO HER DAUGHTER, 1904

*John Wallace Riddle*, c. 1921

Harris Ewing,
Washington, D.C.,
Photographer

Archives,
Hill-Stead Museum

# John Wallace Riddle

*Philadelphia, Pennsylvania, July 12, 1864 –*
*Farmington, Connecticut, December 8, 1941*

John Wallace Riddle's father died before his son's birth. When he was seven his mother married Judge Charles Flandrau of St. Paul, Minnesota, a widower with two daughters. The couple had two sons together. Although John funded his own education from a small inheritance, his step-father's important political connections helped advance his diplomatic career. After graduating from Harvard in 1886, John attended Columbia Law School and then the École des Sciences et Politiques in Paris. He became a skilled linguist proficient in six languages. His diplomatic posts included Turkey, Egypt, Romania, Russia and Argentina. He met Theodate in 1905 through their mutual friend and Farmington resident Anna Roosevelt Cowles, Theodore Roosevelt's sister. John and Theodate married in 1916. During World War I, he worked for the Army War College. If John and Theodate's marriage was a relationship based partly on mutual convenience, it also was af-fection-ate. She called him "Totem" because of his height, and he called her "Dearest of Geniuses."

"[John] certainly is of sufficient maturity to 'know his own mind,' and while...it seems to me as a rule inadvisable for a very poor man to marry a very rich woman, it often works entirely well."

—CHARLES FLANDRAU, RIDDLE'S HALF-BROTHER, TO A RELATIVE, JANUARY, 1916

## Earnest Bohlen

*Near Montgomery, Alabama, December 22, 1853 –*
*Farmington, Connecticut, December 11, 1942*

Earnest was born on a plantation in the South.
His African American mother was a seamstress.
His father, a white overseer, was killed in the
Civil War. When Earnest was in his late teens his
mother sent him North to find work. Later, when
the Popes' new house on Euclid Avenue in
Cleveland was completed, probably around 1885,
Alfred and Ada hired Earnest as their butler, a
position he held until the end of his life. He man-
aged domestic affairs at Hill-Stead, oversaw the
household staff, and greeted and tended to the
needs of visitors. Friends and relatives enjoyed his
gentle presence as much as the family did. When
Earnest died at 90, Theodate had him buried in
the family plot in Farmington.

*Earnest Bohlen,* 1931
John Haley, Photographer
Archives, Hill-Stead Museum

"His association with the

family was always—shall I say,

'relaxed reserve.' Everybody

loved him dearly."

—DONALD CARSON, THEODATE POPE RIDDLE'S
FOSTER SON, REMEMBERING EARNEST, 1996

# Alfred Atmore Pope, An American Collector

## "I believe I have the best— the finest—Degas and Manet in America."

—ALFRED POPE, 1894

*Alfred Atmore Pope, age 21,* c. 1865

Archives, Hill-Stead Museum

In collecting art, Alfred Atmore Pope was passionate and discerning. His penchant for Impressionist paintings, in their immediacy and boldness, distinguished him within a select group of connoisseurs at the turn of the 20th century. Alfred made a radical departure from the traditional tastes of many of his peers who acquired only Old Master paintings and drawings. Favoring quality over quantity, he took home the best works of art, not the most. Today, Alfred Pope's Impressionist collection at Hill-Stead Museum contains singular examples by Manet, Monet and Degas.

Alfred did not limit his collecting to Impressionism alone. He acquired mainstream paintings in the officially sanctioned academic style of Pierre Puvis de Chavannes, as well as numerous decorative arts objects, including bronze sculpture and Asian and European porcelains, and Asian, American and European prints—etchings, mezzotints and woodblocks.

## The Business Years

Alfred Pope epitomized the self-made man, keenly entrepreneurial and opportunistic. He married Ada Brooks, his childhood sweetheart, in 1866, and worked alongside his father and brothers in the family woolen business. In 1869 he secured loans from his brother-in-law, Joshua Brooks, and others, and bought into and became secretary and treasurer of the newly formed Cleveland Malleable Iron Company. Within ten years, at the age of 37, he rose to the rank of president.

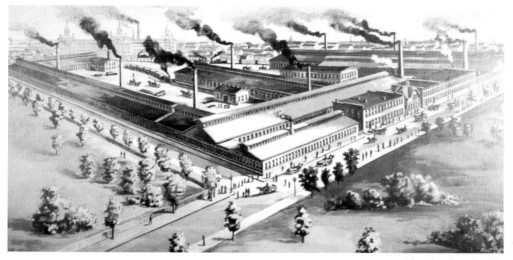

*Cleveland Malleable Iron Company,* c. 1886

Archives, Hill-Stead Museum

Early on, Pope and his associates were guided by the experience of J. H. Whittemore, president of a thriving malleable iron concern in Naugatuck, Connecticut. The Cleveland firm prospered, relying on its manufacture of malleable iron, an exceptionally strong form of metal, much stronger than forged iron and of great use in the burgeoning railroad industry. The company made acquisitions and became the Malleable Castings Company in 1891. Through perseverance and sound investment Pope became comfortable financially, wealthy by some standards. As his company grew, he moved his family up the ladder of Cleveland society and eventually built a Queen Anne-style townhouse on Euclid Avenue in one of the city's most fashionable districts. John D. Rockefeller was among his neighbors.

After 32 years in industry, Pope and his wife retired to Farmington, Connecticut, where their only child, daughter Theodate, was living. At Hill-Stead he became a gentleman farmer, and with his daughter developed a dairy business.

During retirement, Pope remained active in business but took time out for favorite pastimes—baseball and golf. He attended games and played golf regularly at Hill-Stead on his personal six-hole golf grounds conveniently located just down the hill from his study.

*Alfred and Ada Pope and daughter Theodate arrive at their new home, c. 1902*

Gertrude Käsebier, Photographer

Alfred Atmore Pope Collection, Hill-Stead Museum

## The Grand Tour

Pope's interest in French Impressionist art began in 1888-1889 when he took Ada and Theodate on a European Grand Tour. Harris Whittemore, the son of Pope's colleague, joined them periodically throughout the tour. Harris, himself, became a notable collector of Impressionist art.[6] The two friends exchanged opinions and news about art for 25 years, until Pope's death in 1913.

During their travels, Alfred, Ada, Theodate and Harris visited such museums as the Louvre and the Luxembourg Palace in Paris, where they saw seminal works by French, Italian and Spanish masters. They galvanized their knowledge of the contemporary art scene, however, through visits to Parisian galleries and relationships with art dealers. The best known and most influential Parisian dealer at the time was Paul Durand-Ruel, who conducted a high-quality commercial sales operation, published art journals and maintained a private collection for exhibition. Durand-Ruel's gallery was the ideal classroom—intimate and dynamic—for a self-educated and self-made member of the new bourgeoisie, such as Alfred Pope.

A few days after their arrival in Paris, the Popes visited Durand-Ruel at the suggestion of Ada Pope's brother, Edward

---

[6] While the Pope collection remains intact, the Whittemore collection does not.

(Ned) Brooks, an artist living and working in Paris. Theodate frequently accompanied her father on gallery visits, and her diary entries track the evolution of the family's opinions about Impressionist art. Theodate's journal entry describing their first gallery visit reveals naiveté and even skepticism:

> This morning we all, Uncle Ned included went to Mr. Durand-Ruel's house to see his collection of pictures made by impression-ists. One or two seemed good, the others seemed to me, who cannot appreciate them, just stuff. I think perhaps the men of that school began with a good idea and their pic-tures are certainly fresh in style, but when they offer us a canvas that we cannot tell if the painting is meant to represent water or a field I think to say the least they are off. I wonder if some men do not depend on this coming craze to make inexcusable pictures and to sell them to the uninstructed (or fools) as samples of this new school.[7]

*Alfred Atmore Pope aboard ship,* c. 1890

Archives, Hill-Stead Museum

Gradually, the Popes warmed to the Impressionists. By the time the family returned to Paris in May of 1889, they had traveled extensively in Spain, Italy and England, visiting museums and galleries, including an Impressionist exhibi-tion in London.[8] Shortly after they arrived in Paris, they vis-ited the Salon, a major exhibition of "significant" artists that had opened on May 1. Theodate's diary entry of May 9, 1889 reflects a cautious reversal of her earlier position:

> Now the impressionists are interesting, but I doubt if any of the work they are doing now will last. It has its place in the history of art because they came at just the right time. They are showing us that nature should be studied out of doors & that no landscape ought to be painted in the studio. The[y] are bringing us a freshness that Corot, Rousseau, Daubigny and others

[7] Theodate Pope Diary, November 9, 1888, Archives, Hill-Stead Museum.
[8] Theodate Pope Diary, April 16, 1889, Archives, Hill-Stead Museum.

never dreamed of. Nevertheless they are going too far in the opposite direction but still it takes some men to go beyond the line to bring others to it or as Papa says the impressionists are shouting in order to be heard. The wise men will follow them only they will go slowly and never go quite as far.[9]

*Hill-Stead's Drawing Room,* c. 1902

*Grainstacks, White Frost Effect* hangs above fireplace and *The Guitar Player* hangs above piano

*The Architectural Review,* vol. 9, November, 1902

Archives, Hill-Stead Museum

A few days after Theodate wrote these thoughts, her father purchased his first Impressionist painting, Monet's *View of Cap d'Antibes*, 1888, which reflects the brilliant light and color of the Mediterranean coast. Perhaps a recent visit to Cap d'Antibes prompted Pope to conclude that Monet had captured the scene's essence in a new and exciting manner; this oil was a fitting selection for a forward-thinking businessman on the cutting edge of collecting art.

Upon their third return to Paris after further travels on the continent, Theodate proclaimed that she was "growing enthusiastic over Monet." On August 16, 1889, the family saw one of Monet's haystacks or grainstacks in an exhibition at Petit's Gallery. This was a decisive moment in their rapidly maturing appreciation of the Impressionists. In a few short months, Theodate had gone from virtual indifference to passionately espousing its rhetoric. On August 23, 1889 she wrote:

[9] Theodate Pope Diary, May 9, 1889, Archives, Hill-Stead Museum.

*Hill-Stead's Dining Room,* c. 1909

*Grainstacks, in Bright Sunlight* hangs above sideboard

*American Homes and Gardens,* vol. VII, no. 2, February, 1910

Archives, Hill-Stead Museum

Mr. Vinton [an American artist] does not like the Impressionist school as Papa and I do. I think they have something new to say and I also think that it is well worth paying attention to. Did men of any other school ever paint sunlight as the Impressionists do? No! But I don't blame them for not doing it—not at all. But I do think we ought to show our appreciation and herald in such men as Monet and De Gaz [sic].[10]

Clearly, Pope was won over as well. He came home with three paintings by Monet, including *View of Cap d'Antibes,* 1888, and *Grainstacks, White Frost Effect,* 1889.

While on the Grand Tour, Pope and his daughter grew closer, conversing about art and Theodate's future. Pope was perhaps an unconventional 19th-century father in that he actively encouraged his daughter to pursue a career. He fostered her creativity during her childhood and adolescence by providing for art lessons. While traveling he encouraged Theodate to pursue her interests in architecture.

*Alfred Pope and daughter Theodate on holiday in Maine,* c. 1905

Archives, Hill-Stead Museum

[10] Theodate Pope Diary, August 23, 1889, Archives, Hill-Stead Museum.

## Artistic Pursuits

In 1894, during a four-month sojourn in Europe, the Popes acquired Monet's *Fishing Boats at Sea*, 1868, and Manet's *The Guitar Player*, 1866. Alfred paid a record sum of $12,000 for the latter, prompting the artist Camille Pissarro to observe:

> I met Collard in Paris, he told me the story of this American who came to Paris to find a beautiful Manet and was willing to pay any price if the painting met his expectations. All the dealers were exhausted from continual searching in every corner for the pearl. Finally this nabob purchased the *Woman With Guitar* from Durand-Ruel for 75,000 francs. Amazement far and wide.[11]

During this trip Pope also began collecting works by the American expatriate artist, James McNeill Whistler. His first purchase was *The Blue Wave, Biarritz*, 1862, and later that year, *Symphony in Violet and Blue*, 1893. His correspondence of that period reveals a growing conviction of taste:

> I was taken with "The Blue Wave" it seemed & seems *masterful*—It's about the size of a large Monet—in style it's very like a Courbet—which used to be at the Luxemburg (now at the Louvre the color is different—blue instead of green—the waves more natural *not* suggesting *tapestry* & yet far from the photographic sea of Henry Moore)—There is the *big* feeling of the ocean similar to Courbet.[12]

In an 1894 letter to Harris Whittemore, Pope describes in dramatic detail a lunch he had at Giverny as Monet's guest.[13] He observes that the "salmon pink and white dresses" of Monet's daughters and the green of Mme. Monet's dress "*all* made fine

---

[11] John Rewald, *Camille Pissaro Letters to His Son Lucien*. New York: Pantheon Books, Inc., 1943.

[12] Alfred Pope letter to Harris Whittemore, August 26, 1894, Archives, Hill-Stead Museum and Whittemore Trust Collection.

[13] Alfred Pope letter to Harris Whittemore, August 25, 1894, Archives, Hill-Stead Museum and Whittemore Trust Collection. All the quotations in the entire paragraph are taken from this letter.

color effect." He describes the dining room as "a symphony of yellows." Pope mentions the luscious aquatic garden, the dining room and hall "just hung *full* of Japanese prints in quiet little frames," and the artist's house and offices "are hung with pictures like paper on the wall." It is clear that Pope's sensibilities were attuned to the subtleties of color, value and composition. Finally, Pope sums up the artist: "Monet strikes you as sturdy & strong in physique & intellect—a fine soft-brown eye—one that sees everything—A lovely smile—a *clever* man—you wouldn't take him for an artist—more like a business man turned from town to country." Coming from Pope, a businessman himself, this was high praise.

In addition to collecting in Europe, Pope acquired Impressionist pieces from dealers in New York City. The Popes maintained a residence at the Windsor Hotel on Fifth Avenue in Manhattan[14] and frequently journeyed there for business and pleasure. Durand-Ruel of Paris had opened a branch office in New York in 1886 and often arranged special visits for the Popes, such as the viewing of two private collections in Philadelphia.[15] On one of Durand-Ruel's trip to the United States in 1893, he visited the Popes at their home in Cleveland. In a brief letter to Harris Whittemore, Pope jokes that Durand-Ruel would have enjoyed the pictures more if Pope had bought them all from Durand-Ruel, himself.[16]

## Education and Influence

When he purchased a work that did not meet his standards or, perhaps, did not fit with the other works in his collection,

---

[14] The Windsor Hotel was located on 5th Avenue between 46th and 47th Street. The hotel was destroyed by fire on St. Patrick's Day, March 17, 1899.
[15] Alfred Pope letter to J. H. Whittemore, December 17, 1892 notes: "Spent Thursday in Philadelphia visiting two private picture collections, being personally conducted by Mr. Glenzer of New York." Archives, Hill-Stead Museum and Whittemore Trust Collection.
[16] Alfred Pope letter to Harris Whittemore, November 11, 1893, Archives, Hill-Stead Museum and Whittemore Trust Collection.

Pope was quick to exchange it. He brought to his collecting the same decisiveness and independence of spirit that characterized his business dealings. He was both a rugged individualist, relying on his own judgment, and like all collectors, strongly influenced by the trends of his time. A select few helped guide his choices, including Edward (Ned) Brooks, family friend Clinton Peters, and artists James McNeill Whistler and Mary Cassatt. None of these individuals, however, assumed the role of official advisor.

Both Ned Brooks and Clinton Peters, a relative of the Whittemore family, lived in Paris in the late 1880s and early 1890s and considered themselves artists, though neither achieved commercial or critical success. Brooks introduced Pope to Paul Durand-Ruel in 1888 and later provided him with news from the Parisian art scene. In 1891, he wrote: "Monet is out with a new landscape, Haystacks; something like yours, only not winter, but bathed in the warm morning light of an autumn day. It is truly a wonderful picture; incomprehensible as usual to the ordinary, but nevertheless a great picture. They ask 5,000 francs. His prices are advancing."[17] This same year Pope purchased his second Monet from the grainstack series. Clinton Peters acted as art agent for the Whittemore family and accompanied Pope to various galleries in Paris in 1894.

Mary Cassatt influenced the formation of numerous American collections, including that of H. O. and Louisine Havemeyer, which today makes up a substantial portion of the Impressionist holdings at the Metropolitan Museum of Art in New York. A friend of the Popes, Cassatt did not officially advise them. In fact, in 1894 Pope thanked Harris for forwarding a letter from Cassatt, but continued, "I don't think I can make up my mind to trouble her."[18] In another letter, he commented:

[17] Edward Brooks to Alfred Pope, May 1891, W-768, Archives, Hill-Stead Museum and Whittemore Trust Collection.
[18] Alfred Pope to Harris Whittemore, August 26, 1894, Archives, Hill-Stead Museum and Whittemore Trust Collection.

**Dining Room**
*Jockeys,* 1886, by Edgar Degas hangs above mantle

Jerry L. Thompson, Photographer

**Drawing Room** with view through arch into **Entry Hall**
*Grainstacks, White Frost Effect,* 1889, by Claude Monet hangs above sofa
Jerry L. Thompson, Photographer

**Drawing Room**
*The Tub,* 1886, by Edgar Degas hangs above commode
*View of Cap d'Antibes,* 1888, by Claude Monet hangs above mantle
Jerry L. Thompson, Photographer

**Ell Room**

*Peace,* c. 1861, by Pierre Puvis de Chavannes hangs above desk

Jerry L. Thompson, Photographer

View into **Second Library**
*The Blue Wave, Biarritz,* 1862, by James McNeill Whistler hangs above mantle
Jerry L. Thompson, Photographer

**Claude Monet** (French, 1840-1926)
*Fishing Boats at Sea,* 1868
Oil on canvas, 37½ x 50¾ inches

**Claude Monet** (French, 1840-1926)
*Grainstacks, White Frost Effect,* 1889
Oil on canvas, 25¼ x 36 inches

**Edgar Hillaire Degas** (French, 1834-1917)
*The Tub*, 1886
Pastel on paper, 27½ x 27½ inches

**Edgar Hillaire Degas** (French, 1834-1917)
*Dancers In Pink,* c. 1876
Oil on canvas, 23¼ x 29¼ inches

**Édouard Manet** (French, 1832-1883)
*The Guitar Player,* 1866
Oil on canvas, 25 x 31½ inches

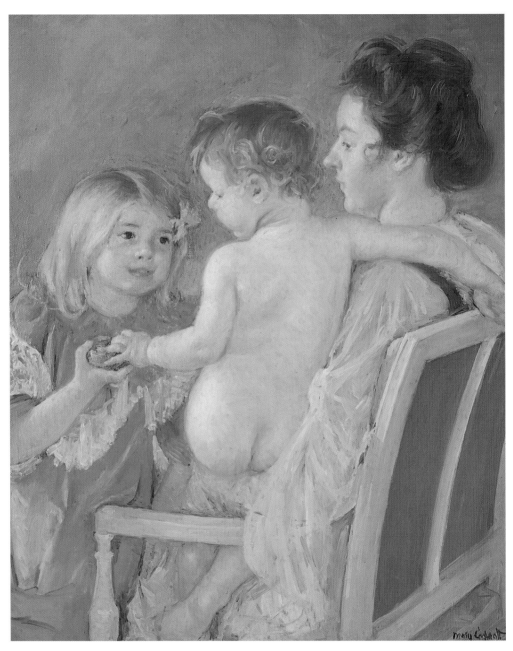

**Mary Cassatt** (American, 1844-1926)
*Sara Handing a Toy to the Baby,* c. 1901
Oil on canvas, 33 x 27 inches

...I have been wavering about ordering the pastel. I hardly think I will do so, it is such a game of chance; although I know this picture has the endorsement of Miss Cassatt, and I am so much impressed by its simplicity. Of course, if it were an oil at that price, I should not hesitate; then again I am influenced by the fact that I sometimes think I am a little reckless.[19]

Cassatt may have influenced Pope indirectly in his purchase of the Degas' *The Tub*. He probably saw a similar painting by the same artist, *Woman Bathing in a Shallow Tub*, hanging in Cassatt's own apartment on one of his visits.[20]

Pope's relationship with Whistler blossomed after he purchased *The Blue Wave, Biarritz* on his 1894 European trip. Although it is clear that Pope both valued and respected Whistler's suggestions, he was selective about what advice he acted upon. In a letter to Pope about two paintings, one of them *Nocturne in Gray and Gold: Chelsea Snow* (Fogg Art Museum, Harvard University, Cambridge, Massachusetts), Whistler wrote:

I was of course pleased with all that you tell me in your letter—of course now that you have begun, you will become a collector of "Blue"! ... Goupil has two of my pictures for sale! ...if you have not already seen them, go—and certainly, if you are at all inclined to act on your brother-in-law's theory of "buying all Whistlers," you ought to have a try for the Nocturne *Grey and Gold—Chelsea Snow*—you will find it in Miss Theodate's catalogue (No. 13). It is a beauty... I should be delighted to know that the picture left that country, to find its home among its fellows in your good care and sympathy![21]

Pope's response:

[19] Alfred Pope to Harris Whittemore, March 15, 1894, Archives, Hill-Stead Museum and Whittemore Trust Collection.
[20] Ibid. Hirshler 184, painting now in the collection of the Metropolitan Museum of Art, New York.
[21] James McNeill Whistler to Alfred Pope, no date but it was in the fall of 1894 before September 22, 1894, Archives, Hill-Stead Museum.

Yes I have seen the two pictures at Goupils. I agree with you in liking the "Chelsea Snow" the best and liking it well too but I cannot live up to Ned Brooks suggestions—I must go home recover my breath and build up to the anticipation of *"the figure piece"* which if unrealized will make me unhappy—you know everything comes to the collector who waits. I believe I have the best—the finest—Degas and Manet in America and I want to over-match them with the finest Whistler—We ought to bring this about— YOU and I.[22]

Although Pope did not follow Whistler's recommendations in this case, he seemed happy enough to let Whistler guide him, accepting his letters of introduction to view works in private collections and to see Whistler's interior design project known as the Peacock Room at the home of Frederick R. Leyland at Prince's Gate in London.

*Alfred Pope relaxes on Hill-Stead's west lawn with dog Silas, c. 1905*

Archives, Hill-Stead Museum

The Alfred Atmore Pope Collection is a testament to one man who developed a personal aesthetic worthy of a scholar. As one of the earliest Americans to collect Impressionist art, he did not rely on the opinions of the past, but instead saw and liked what was fresh and new. The relatively small number of works in his collection reflects his practicality in having only the number of paintings that could comfortably fit into his house. He loved these paintings and enjoyed them every day—as we are privileged to do a century later on visits to Hill-Stead Museum.

---

[22] Alfred Pope to James McNeill Whistler, Archives, Hill-Stead Museum, letters from Pope to Whistler are preserved in the Glasgow University Library, Scotland.

*View of House from main driveway,* 2000

# Tour of the House

 A visit to Hill-Stead is a rich experience. It was architect Theodate Pope Riddle's first masterpiece, originally conceived as a whole work of art inclusive of a family home, working farm and community center. Architecture and landscape are as important as the contents of the house. Visitors explore 19 rooms filled with notable works of art and furnishings amassed by the Pope and Riddle families. These intact domestic interiors, including bathrooms and closets, illustrative of the 1916-1920 period, lack only the original kitchen, laundry and servants quarters.

## Porte-Cochere

House tours begin either here, where vehicles once dropped off guests, or inside the Carriage Porch.

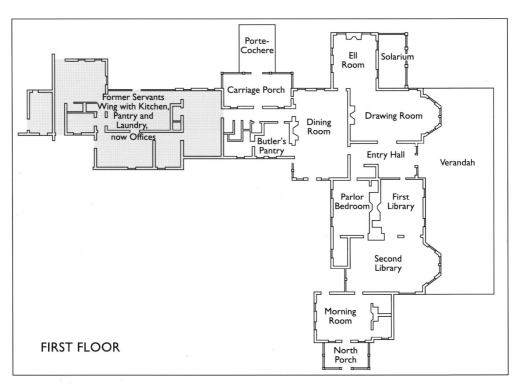

**FIRST FLOOR**

Porte-Cochere

Ell Room

Solarium

Carriage Porch

Drawing Room

Dining Room

Butler's Pantry

Entry Hall

Verandah

Former Servants Wing with Kitchen, Pantry and Laundry, now Offices

Parlor Bedroom

First Library

Second Library

Morning Room

North Porch

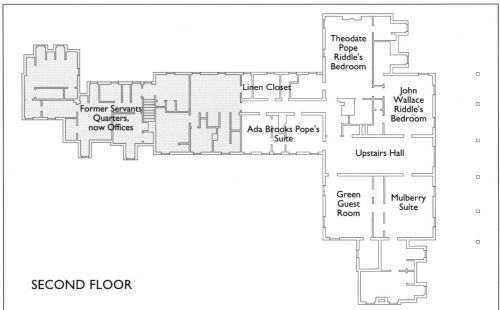

**SECOND FLOOR**

Theodate Pope Riddle's Bedroom

Linen Closet

John Wallace Riddle's Bedroom

Former Servants Quarters, now Offices

Ada Brooks Pope's Suite

Upstairs Hall

Green Guest Room

Mulberry Suite

**FLOOR PLAN**

## Carriage Porch

During warm months when the Popes and Riddles were in residence (1901-1946), screens replaced window glass and this porch became a pleasant room for dining. Today, visitors stand within this sun drenched space and look through 219 panes of glass to a landscape of trees, stonewalls and gardens.

## Dining Room

Dining Room

Visitors pass through an oversized Dutch door into Hill-Stead's largest room. Over the fireplace hangs *Jockeys*, a pastel from 1886 by Edgar Degas. The Popes exhibited their celadon green Chinese porcelains on the mantle and selected the wool carpet to complement the vivid green that dominates the *Jockeys*. Tucked into a corner in its original frame is *Symphony in Violet and Blue* (1893), an oil painting by American expatriate artist James McNeill Whistler. Family portraits further distinguish the room.

The American Federal-style dining table, which when fully extended seats 30 people, was illuminated by two elaborately ornamented gas chandeliers. All of Hill-Stead's original chandeliers and wall sconces were converted from gas to electricity as soon as electric lines made their way into Farmington in the early 1900s.

The American Empire mahogany sideboard (1815-1840) displays two English 18th-century urn-shaped knife boxes and crystal decanters. The majority of the furniture is Federal in style and includes a card table, drop leaf table, two sofas, a pair of satinwood cabinets and the large break-front cabinet that displays English, American, German and French silver from the 18th and 19th centuries. The room's paneling, painted to resemble oak graining, was a decorative touch found in both Colonial and Colonial Revival houses. The wallpaper, hand-block printed in France for an American company, includes mythological references and decorative swags.

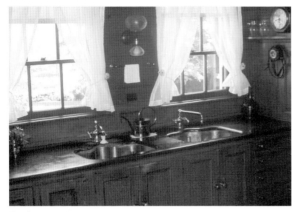

Butler's Pantry

## Butler's Pantry

The Butler's Pantry, the domain of Earnest Bohlen, was a holding area for meals and connected the "working" part of the house— kitchen, secondary pantry, scullery, laundry and staff quarters—to the formal rooms. A warming oven, nickel silver sinks, iceboxes, grain bins, numerous cabinets and a two-toned rubber floor represent Theodate's fascination with modernity and dedication to function. Blue and white porcelain, commonly called Cantonware, occupies the open shelves. A large Connecticut-made combination safe securely stored the family's silver flatware and other valuables.

Entry Hall

## Entry Hall

Period photographs confirm that this space remains nearly as it was in 1901. The wallpaper is an original brick-and-scrollwork pattern with floral accents. Furnishings include an Empire sofa and marble-topped pier table, card table, Pembroke table and Scottish tall case clock.

# Drawing Room

Family and friends retired after dinner to the Drawing Room, "parlor" or "living room" to talk, play cards or listen to music played on the family's 1901 custom-made Steinway grand piano. The boxed-beamed ceiling and butterscotch-colored woodwork convey Colonial era warmth and intimacy, yet the scale of the room is grand. Here the Popes chose to display inspiring masterpieces: Monet's *Grainstacks, White Frost Effect* (1889) and *View of Cap d'Antibes* (1888), Degas' *Dancers in Pink* (c. 1876), and Édouard Manet's *The Guitar Player* (1866) and *Toreadors* (1863).

Among the furnishings are fine examples of 19th-century English, American and Irish Chippendale-style. On each side of the fireplace sit late 18th-century French marquetry commodes with marble tops and

Drawing Room

ormolu mountings. Objects include Japanese *netsuke* and *inro*, stone chops and several Chinese vases; three 18th-century English tea caddies with marquetry shell designs; a bronze sculpture of a lion and serpent by the French sculptor Antoine-Louis Barye; several pieces of late 19th- and early 20th-century Italian maiolica; two 17th-century Abruzzian maiolica urns and a 16th-century bowl from Urbino.

# Ell Room

The Popes enjoyed this intimate extension of the Drawing Room when they were alone. Monet's *Grainstacks, in Bright*

37

*Sunlight* (1890) hangs above the mantle, complemented by an oxblood glaze Chinese porcelain vase from the K'ang Hsi period of the Ch'ing Dynasty (1661-1722); 19th-century English pink lusterware goblets; a bracket clock by Ralph Gout, London (c. 1780); and a bronze lioness by Barye. The Federal-style mahogany sewing table is unusual for a pouch made of wood rather than fabric. An American William and Mary-style gate leg table can be found here and in many rooms throughout Hill-Stead. A small oil painting, *Peace* (c. 1861), by the French artist Pierre Puvis de Chavannes,[23] hangs above the desk.

First Library

## First Library

This paneled and book-lined room contains a comfortable German Biedermeier sofa of cherry, upholstered in silk brocade (1820-1850), and a caned armchair with a reading arm bracket. The library reflects the family's eclectic interests, ranging from art history and architecture to botany, world history, psychic phenomena, religion and social concerns, poetry and fiction. A group of 18th- and 19th-century mezzotints, prints made after English portraits, hang over the fireplace. A Swiss-made tortoise shell and gilt clock (c. 1800) complements oxblood glaze Chinese porcelain on the mantle.

## Second Library

Above the fireplace hangs *The Blue Wave, Biarritz* (1862) by James McNeill Whistler, one of Pope's favorite acquisitions.

[23] Detail from a pair of grand murals entitled *War and Peace*, originally exhibited in the Salon of 1861, now hanging in the Musée Picardie, Amiens, France.

On the mantle are a Corinthian pyxis jar, dated 600-575 BCE, the oldest object in the house, and a piece of Chinese pottery from the Han Dynasty (206 BCE-220 CE). In 1906-1907, Theodate designed an addition to the home, including a bay window that expanded this room toward the Verandah, and

Second Library

linked the Libraries by two wide openings that feature an innovative four-sided bookshelf column. Furnishings include two American Empire mahogany sofas with wing and claw feet and a bombe-front mahogany china cabinet that holds the Popes' large collection of English lusterware.

## Morning Room

When Theodate expanded the Second Library, she added this room as a study for her father. From the North Porch, he could access his six-hole golf grounds. Monet's *Fishing Boats at Sea* (1868) dominates the room. In the 1930s Theodate redecorat-

Morning Room

ed the space and began using it as her sitting room and office. Appointments include 19th-century architectural prints of London, Oxford, Edinburgh and other British and European cities. A mahogany secretary with architectural motifs, including a paneled door, brickwork and fluted pilasters, also reflects her abiding interest in architecture.

Parlor Bedroom

## Parlor Bedroom

Most often used as a lounge for guests, this room's focal point is a massive early 19th-century American mahogany four-poster bed, probably made in Massachusetts. Typical for Hill-Stead, an American 19th-century sewing table serves as a nightstand. Furnishings include a secretary and bookcase, this one a copy after the 18th-century English cabinetmaker Thomas Chippendale; Chinese-inspired fretwork adorns the drawers and top. The mantle boasts a 19th-century lyre-shaped clock with a rhinestone pendulum in the style of French King Louis XVI and fine examples of blue and white Chinese Ming and Ch'ing Dynasty porcelains. Three mirrors add to the room's grandeur, one of Venetian etched glass in the Rococo-style, another in English Federal-style, and a third, American Empire-style gilt. *Head of a Woman* (c. 1890), by Eugène Carrière hangs to the right of the fireplace.

Stairway and Upper Hall

## Stairway and Upper Hall

Filling the wall of the Stairway are 36 framed prints by such notable 18th- and 19th-century artists as Giovanni Battista Piranesi, James McNeill Whistler and Jean Francois Millet. In the Upper Hall are works by William Nicholson,[24]

[24] William Nicholson (British, 1872-1949) *Morris Dancers at the Gates of Blenheim*, 1903, oil on canvas, 23 x 21 inches.

Albrecht Dürer[25] and Eugène Carrière. A c. 1780 French clock hangs between c. 1935 portraits of Theodate Pope Riddle and her husband John Wallace Riddle, painted from photographs by artists at the C. J. Fox Studio in New York.

## Green Guest Room

Complete with amenities to ensure the comfort of guests—a private bathroom, a mahogany writing desk in the Federal-style and a late 17th-century oak chest of drawers from England—this room boasts two works of art by Mary Cassatt, the oil *Sara Handing a Toy to the Baby* (c. 1901) and an aquatint, *Gathering Fruit* (1893).

Green Guest Room

## Mulberry Suite

Like the Green Guest Room, the Mulberry Suite takes its name from the room's dominant color.

Mulberry Suite

With its two bedrooms and connecting bath, massive four-poster bed and comfortable seating, this suite would have been a welcome sight to any traveling family. Portraits of John Wallace Riddle's ancestors, by anonymous American artists, decorate the walls.

[25] Albrecht Dürer (German, 1471-1528) *Madonna Crowned by Two Angels* (c. 1518) engraving, 3⅞ x 5⅛ inches; *The Rape of Anemone* or *The Sea Monster* (c. 1498) engraving, 7½ x 10 inches; and *Melencholia I* (1514) engraving, 7½ x 9½ inches.

## John Wallace Riddle's Bedroom

After she and John wed in 1916, Theodate connected this former guest room to the master bedroom next door by converting a closet into a passageway.

John Wallace Riddle's Bedroom

Personal effects on display include portraits of John's maternal grandparents by the Philadelphia artist Thomas Sully (1782-1872), a small selection of travel books and the Japanese *hapi* coats he and Theodate purchased as souvenirs on a trip to Asia in 1919.

## Theodate Pope Riddle's Bedroom

Originally occupied by Alfred and Ada Pope, Theodate and John made the larger space into a master suite with dressing room, walk-in closet and an oversized bathroom, complete

Theodate Pope Riddle's Bedroom

with foot tub and plentiful built-in cabinets. The closet displays some of Theodate's garments, hats and her made-to-order Tiffany & Co. traveling case, a gift from her father in 1889. Photographs of loved ones are on the secretary, dresser, mantle and bedside table.

## Ada Brooks Pope's Suite

Once used by Theodate when she was a guest at Hill-Stead, this cozy suite became Ada's quarters after her daughter's marriage in 1916. The sitting room reflects Ada and Alfred

Pope's passion for Japanese woodblock prints, among them seven works by Hokusai (1760-1849), including two of his *36 Views of Mt. Fuji* series;[26] ten prints by Hiroshige (1797-1858), including four from his *53 Stations of the Tokaido* series;[27] and five by Utamaro

Mrs. Pope's Suite

(1750-1806), including *Passionate Woman*.[28] The adjoining bedroom contains a canopied bed and three woodblock prints by Hokusai.

## Linen Room and Servants Quarters

Across the hall from Ada's bedroom, the compactly constructed linen room is the model of efficiency, with many built-in cupboards and drawers and a sewing station. At the end of the hallway, a door leads into the service wing, now converted to museum offices. The original servants rooms were small, often equipped with sinks; household staff members shared tub rooms and water closets. Butler Earnest Bohlen lived in private quarters and had his own full bathroom.

Linen Closet

[26] *The Great Wave* is the most well known.
[27] The most recognized of the series is *Driving Rain at Shono*.
[28] From his series on the *Ten Physiognomic Aspects of Women*.

## Sunken Garden

The Sunken Garden is set into a natural depression and sur-rounded by rustic dry laid stone walls. A summer house marks the center of an octagonal-shaped space further defined by enclosing yew hedges. Thirty-six flowerbeds contain nearly 90 plant varieties. Warren Manning, advised Theodate on Hill-Stead's overall landscape design, including this garden.

Sunken Garden and Summer House

Beatrix Jones Farrand, a noted American garden designer and niece of author Edith Wharton, created the Sunken Garden planting plan c. 1920. She selected varieties for con-tinuous bloom throughout the growing season and used colors that complement the Impressionist paintings inside the house. The garden is something of a miracle, having been seeded over during World War II, but re-established in 1986 by mem-bers of the Connecticut Valley Garden Club and the Garden Club of Hartford. These local volunteers were aided by the serendipitous discovery of the original Farrand planting plan, on which the designer noted: "for the garden of Mrs. J. W. Riddle, Farmington, Conn." Today museum staff and a core of dedicated volunteers maintain the garden.

# Highlights of the Alfred Atmore Pope Collection

Visitors touring the interiors at Hill-Stead see Alfred Atmore Pope's prized collection of French Impressionist paintings and much more. Highlights are described here. The museum's archives include Theodate's diaries, household and business documents, and receipts for the purchase of artwork. Correspondence from Mary Cassatt, Henry James and James McNeill Whistler are among 13,000 letters and postcards. Among approximately 2,500 photographs dating from 1885-1946, are six of Gertrude Käsebier's "art" photographs and a dozen other images she took of Pope family members. Hill-Stead's archives are open to researchers by appointment.

## **Eugène Carrière** (French, 1849-1906)

The grandson and nephew of artists, Carrière began his career as a commercial lithographer. This early experience with printmaking contributed to the dark, monochromatic coloring of the bulk of his work, although *Head of a Woman*, with its vivid red flower, is characteristic of his early paintings. This image almost certainly depicts the artist's wife, Sophie. Artists and critics alike hailed Carrière as a genius. He was popular with 19th-century art collectors. Theodate's Grand Tour diary entry of May 11, 1889, mentions that her father purchased another Carrière, a "portrait of a baby," from Goupil's, Paris. Hill-Stead exhibits two other Carrière paintings: *Maternity*, c. 1880 and *Child at Table*, c. 1880, both of which appear to feature one or the other son, Jean-Rene or Leon.

*Head of a Woman*, c. 1890

Oil on canvas, 16½ x 13¼ inches

*Sara Handing a Toy to the Baby,* c. 1901

Oil on canvas,
33 x 27 inches

## Mary Cassatt (American, 1844-1926)

Mary Cassatt lived most of her adult life in France and was closely aligned with the French Impressionists. She was particularly influenced by Edgar Degas. The Popes were guests in her homes in Paris and the French countryside, and Cassatt visited the family at Hill-Stead on her final trip to the United States in 1908. Two of the six works by Cassatt that the Popes acquired remain in the collection. These include an oil painting, *Sara Handing a Toy to the Baby,* and an aquatint *Gathering Fruit,* both purchased through the influential art dealer Durand-Ruel in Paris. The oil is a prime example of Cassatt's portraits of women and children engaged in domestic activities, casually presented, as opposed to formally posed. The aquatint is from a series that Cassatt created after viewing a groundbreaking exhibition of Japanese graphic arts in Paris in 1890, a show that exerted great influence on Parisian artistic circles. Pope paid just $25 for *Gathering Fruit.*

## Edgar Hillaire Degas (French, 1834-1917)

Degas so favored the ballet that he created about 1,500 works in a variety of media, depicting all aspects of dance—preparation, rehearsal, waiting in the wings, as in *Dancers in Pink,* and the performance itself. The then-burgeoning art of photography, with images conveying a sense of immediacy, influenced both the artist's choice of subject matter and composition. *Dancers in Pink* draws the viewer backstage, catching one's eye with a central bright spot of paint representing a dancer's earring. Pope purchased this painting for $5,000 from Cottier & Co. in New York. It previously belonged to the noted American collector Erwin Davis, who acquired it from art dealer Durand-Ruel's personal collection. This was one of the first Degas paintings to be publicly exhibited in the United States.

Surely Theodate had *Jockeys* in mind when she designed Hill-Stead's Dining Room, where the pastel has hung since 1901. Here the artist imitated two compositional devices from the Japanese woodblock prints he admired and collected—diagonally placing the horses and riders and cropping the scene at the far left. The pastel's horizontal orientation was also inspired by Japanese art. The theme of horse and rider appears at two different periods in Degas' career. In the 1860s he focused on the action of the racecourse; in the 1880s his subject was one of aesthetic contemplation. Pope purchased *Jockeys* from Durand-Ruel, New York, in 1892.

*Dancers In Pink,*
c. 1876

Oil on canvas,
23¼ x 29 inches

*Jockeys,* 1886

Pastel on paper,
15¼ x 34¾ inches

*The Tub,* 1886

Pastel on paper,
27½ x 27½ inches

The finest Degas in the collection, this pastel was Alfred Pope's last Impressionist acquisition. He bought *The Tub* from Durand-Ruel, Paris, in 1907. Degas created the drawing for the eighth and final Impressionist exhibition in Paris, where it was featured with approximately 12 other works in his Salon de Nude. Notable for its size and high degree of finish, the work has an unusually elevated perspective that allows the viewer to voyeuristically steal a glimpse, as if through a keyhole, of the intimate, everyday scene of a woman bathing. His colors are rich and luminescent, creating an effect that Renoir once described as having the "freshness of fresco." At one time this nude hung discreetly in the Parlor Bedroom.

*The Guitar Player,*
1866

Oil on canvas,
25 x 31½ inches

## Édouard Manet
(French, 1832-1883)

Manet strove to paint in a truly modern manner. Paradoxically, he also wanted to be known as an artist versed in the sanctioned styles of the official Paris Salon. Ultimately, what mattered most to him was painting scenes from contemporary life "in the moment," and to this end he composed simply, applying strong colors in a flat manner that threw harsh, strong illumination on his subjects. *The Guitar Player* features the artist's favorite model, Victorine Meurent, wearing a bright white dress that contrasts dramatically with a dark background. Flashes of color come from her blue hair ribbon, a red cord attached to her guitar and the green and yellow feathers of a nearby parrot. Pope purchased *The Guitar Player* from Durand-Ruel, Paris. He paid a record sum of $12,000, the highest amount yet paid for a Manet and the most Pope, himself, ever paid for a single painting. Manet's *Toreadors* showcases his interest in Spanish themes.

*Toreadors,* 1863

Oil on canvas,
20¼ x 35¼ inches

## Claude Monet
(French, 1840-1926)

This is the earliest of Monet's paintings in Hill-Stead's collection, though it is the last Monet that Pope bought. He acquired it from Durand-Ruel, New York, in 1894. In it, dark silhouettes of three boats provide a striking contrast to the orange sky of early morning or dusk. Monet painted the scene out of doors or *en plein air*. The artist's loose brushwork, use of clear, fresh color, and depiction of bright light prefigure his later Impressionist works. With *Fishing Boats at Sea*, Monet pays homage to Manet, who painted similar boating scenes. Pope was delighted to meet Claude Monet at about the time he purchased this painting. A guest for lunch in Giverny, Pope was struck by the distinctive colors and details with which Monet enhanced and defined his home and studio.

*Fishing Boats at Sea,* 1868

Oil on canvas,
37½ x 50¾ inches

(top) *Grainstacks, White Frost Effect,* 1889

Oil on canvas, 25¼ x 36 inches

(above) *Grainstacks, in Bright Sunlight,* 1890

Oil on canvas, 23 x 38 inches

Monet is famous for his serial haystack or grainstack paintings, executed in his rural Giverny backyard. At mid-career, Monet embarked upon intensive studies, painting a single subject at various times of the day and seasons and on several canvases simultaneously in order to study the effects of changing light. In *Grainstacks, White Frost Effect*, a cool pastel palette and rosy hues depict dawn in late autumn. With *Grainstacks, in Bright Sunlight*, Monet examines the same subject, this time at mid-day in summer with a warmer, more intense color selection. Pope bought both paintings from Boussod & Valadon, Paris, the former in 1889 and the latter in 1891.

*View of Cap d'Antibes* was Pope's first Monet, purchased while on the Grand Tour, 1888-1889, from Boussod & Valadon, Paris. It was a logical choice since the Popes had just toured Antibes in the south of France. In a letter to Harris Whittemore, Pope warms to the work of Monet when he writes, "…was invited to the house of Durand-Ruel to see a collection of 'Monets' the master of this school. I may become educated up to understanding and liking one or two of this man's work." Monet created about 12 different views of Antibes and the surrounding Mediterranean countryside. In the series he grappled with capturing atmospheric effects while retaining the purity and brilliance of color. He noted that one wrong dab of paint could look like a stain of dirt.

## James McNeill Whistler

(American, 1834-1903)

Hill-Stead's collection includes over 20 works by

*View of Cap d'Antibes,* 1888

Oil on canvas, 25¾ x 31¾ inches

James McNeill Whistler, both paintings and prints. Pope purchased the two most significant paintings by Whistler, *The Blue Wave, Biarritz* and *Symphony in Violet and Blue*, from Goupil's (later Boussod & Valadon), London, in 1894. The paintings span 30 years of Whistler's career and reflect his evolution from Realism to a more fluid Impressionistic approach. In the earlier of the two oils, *The Blue Wave*, *Biarritz*, Whistler's subject is identifiable and distinct, but not completely realistically rendered. *Symphony in Violet and Blue* is an abstract and ethereal seascape. Hill-Stead's archives include correspondence between Whistler and Pope that reveals the depth of their friendship and mutual regard.

*The Blue Wave, Biarritz,* 1862

Oil on canvas, 25¾ x 35 inches

*Lion with a Serpent,*
c. 1838

Bronze on marble base,
26 x 36 x 19 inches

## Antoine-Louis Barye
(French, 1796-1875)

Of Hill-Stead's eight Barye bronze sculptures, seven depict cats—lion, panther, domestic house cat—the artist's favorite subject. In striving for realism, Barye studied animals and even participated in dissections to more fully understand their anatomy. He created large commissions for the French nobility, but preferred working on a small scale, marketing these more modest bronzes to middle-class Parisians. American collectors favored his small scale works as well. During the period when Pope actively bought art, these bronze sculptures were, in some instances, more expensive than paintings by the Impressionists. Pope paid $1,200 for his largest Barye bronze, *Lion with a Serpent.* The same receipt from Boussod & Valadon lists a painting by the French Impressionist Camille Pissarro at a mere $300.

Albrecht Dürer
(German, 1471-1528)

*Melencolia I,* 1514

Engraving 9⅜ x 7¼ inches

## American and European Prints

Among the most notable prints in the collection are three engravings by Albrecht Dürer, one from the late 15th century and two from the early 16th century. Other significant prints include 17 copper plate etchings and lithographs by Whistler, whose mastery of the medium was instrumental in reviving the popularity of etching in England, France and America. Many of the landscape prints by Jean-François Millet, Giovanni Battista Piranesi and Seymour Haden depict places that the Popes visited. The family amassed a collection of mezzotint portraits of English statesmen, artists, authors and philosophers. The mezzotint process allowed artists to produce the delicate shading and gray tones that closely mimicked painting and was well suited to portraiture. Mezzotints fell out of favor with collectors with the advent of photographic methods.

## Japanese Color Woodblock Prints

James McNeill Whistler (American, 1834-1903)

*Old Battersea Bridge,* before 1879

Copper plate etching, second state, 7⅞ x 11⅝ inches

Like the Impressionists and other 19th-century collectors, the Popes were fascinated with all things Japanese. Alfred and Ada avidly collected Japanese color woodblock prints. In a letter he wrote while visiting Monet in Giverny, Pope describes the artist's dining room as "…just hung *full* of Japanese prints in quiet little frames." Hill-Stead's collection of color woodblock prints includes particularly choice images, with works by Hokusai, Hiroshige and Utamaro. The woodblock print took hold in Japan in the 16th century

during a period of rapid urbanization when book publication started to flourish. As printed images became more colorful and complex, publishers realized that they could market these images independently from books. Though economical because it resulted in numerous copies of the same print, the woodblock print process was complicated, involving publisher, artist, copyist, carver and printer.

Katsushika Hokusai (Japanese, 1760-1849)

*Under the Wave at Kanagawa (The Great Wave),* early 1830s

Colored woodblock print, 10 x 14½ inches

53

## Chinese Ceramics

The Popes left their mark on Hill-Stead with Chinese porcelains positioned to complement the colors in works of art, carpets and decorative details. In the First Library, for example, the oxblood red in a group of vases corresponds to the colors in a tortoiseshell clock nearby and adds warmth to a room dominated by rich brown and gold tones. The Popes collected pieces from the Han (206 BCE-220 CE), Sung (960-1279) and Ming (1368-1644) Dynasties, as well as 19th-century porcelains, including utilitarian export blue and white Cantonware, commonly associated with the Colonial Revival aesthetic.

Selections from the Popes' Collection of Blue and White Canton (China)

Most pieces from the mid to late 19th century

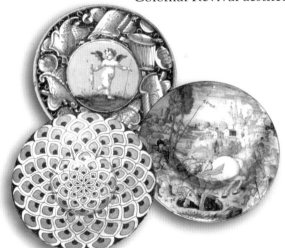

Maiolica Plates
(Italian, 16th century)

## European Ceramics

The Popes purchased numerous plates, urns and jars on their trips abroad. Pieces at Hill-Stead include many fine examples of 16th- and 17th-century Italian maiolica—tin-glazed earthenware pottery noted for its opaque glazing, rich coloring and narrative scenes. Alfred and Ada also collected English lusterware pottery, characterized by an iridescent metallic glaze, usually copper, silver, purple or pink in

color. Their English Wedgwood tea set is executed in a rare yellow-colored porcelain bisque. The
oldest item in the collection is a Corinthian head-
pyxis, c. 600-575 BCE, named for the three female
heads at the top of the jar that serve as handles.
This pyxis, originally used for cosmetics, toilet
articles or jewelry, is the second largest head-pyxis
of only 76 known to exist. It is noteworthy for its
excellent condition and profusion of ornament.

*Jar, Head Pyxis*
(Corinthian,
600-575 BCE)

Earthenware,
9⅛ inches high

## Furnishings

Furnishings at Hill-Stead are primarily Chippendale-style,
Federal-style and Empire, and were purchased by the Popes
specifically for use at Hill-Stead. Sewing and
gate-leg tables are found throughout the house.
Another unifying theme is the inclusion of a
sofa or daybed and secretary in the bedrooms,
along with the typical four-poster bed, bureaus
and gilt framed mirrors. Whereas the furnishings in the Pope's Cleveland house were ornate
Victorian and heavy Arts & Crafts styles, the
furnishings at Hill-Stead are refined and elegant.

## Rugs

The most significant of Hill-Stead's 24 Oriental
rugs range in age from mid-18th century to early
20th century. Three major types—Caucasian,
Persian and Anatolian—come from an area

*Secretary and book-
case* (English, 19th
century)

In the style of
Thomas Chippendale
(1718-1799)

Mahogany,
8 feet 2 inches tall

between the Black Sea and the Persian Gulf. The designs
vary from exquisitely detailed patterns, devised before the
era of mass production, to simpler designs modeled after
European patterns and intended for Western trade. The Popes
collected these rugs for their beauty and function. As a collector, Pope primarily relied on his own judgment, but a

*Rug* (Karabagh, Southern Caucasus Mountain Region- modern day Azerbaijan, late-19th century)

Wool, 4 feet 6 inches x 6 feet 4 inches

letter from James McNeill Whistler steered him toward London shops displaying "beautiful old settings... rugs— baskets and the rest of it."

## Library

Hill-Stead's library contains over 3,300 volumes that belonged to the family. The Popes were a self-educated, well-traveled American family whose reading interests spanned numerous disciplines and several genres. Important volumes include *Noteworthy Paintings in American Private Collections*, edited by artists John LaFarge and August Jaccaci, with a chapter on Alfred Pope's collection; Ogilby's *America* of 1671; and a two-volume 1755 first edition of Samuel Johnson's dictionary. ⌂

Image from early post-card of First and Second Libraries at Hill-Stead

Aerial view of
*Hill-Stead today,*
2001

J. Delano and
W. Wadsworth,
Photographers

# Hill-Stead Time Line

1897        Theodate Pope Riddle meets with Warren
            Manning to plan the site of Hill-Stead.

1898        Alfred Pope begins to purchase land in Farming-
            ton. He acquires 250 acres for his retirement
            home, and instructs Theodate to contact McKim,
            Mead & White to help develop her plan for the
            house and grounds.

1899–1901   Theodate designs and builds Hill-Stead using
            working drawings by Edgerton Swartwout of
            McKim, Mead & White. Richard Jones of
            Farmington is the general contractor. June 16,
            1901, the Popes spend their first night at Hill-
            Stead. Property includes main house, farmhouse,
            shepherd's cottage, stables and garages, hay and
            dairy barns, pump house, sunken garden, wild
            garden, vegetable garden, tennis courts, six-hole
            golf course, orchards, meadows and woodlands.

1902        Theodate adds Mt. Vernon-inspired verandah
            and two years later, a greenhouse and a garage.

1906        Theodate works with McKim, Mead & White to
            add a second library and an office for her father.

57

| | |
|---|---|
| 1907 | Theodate hosts annual meeting of the Connecticut Pomological Society and Dairymen's Association. Hill-Stead's farm is recognized as a model of outstanding agricultural practices. |
| 1908 | Fire destroys stable, laundry and butler's residence. Theodate rebuilds immediately. |
| 1913 | Alfred Pope dies. |
| 1915 | Theodate Pope survives the sinking of the R.M.S. Lusitania. |
| 1916 | Theodate and John Wallace Riddle marry. |
| 1917 | Theodate designs and builds Makeshift Theater and furnishes with graduated wooden benches. She shows films on a silver screen and sponsors community meetings and parties. |
| 1920 | Ada Pope dies. Beatrix Jones Farrand designs planting plan for one-acre Sunken Garden. |
| 1920s | Theodate's Guernsey cow, Anesthesia's Faith, sets world records for high butterfat milk yield. |
| 1941 | John Wallace Riddle dies. |
| 1943 | Earnest Bohlen, beloved butler to the Popes, dies. |
| 1946 | Theodate Pope Riddle dies. Her Last Will and Testament establishes Hill-Stead as a museum. |
| 1947 | Hill-Stead Museum opens to the public. |
| 1986 | Hill-Stead's Sunken Garden is reclaimed with assistance from the Connecticut Valley Garden Club and the Garden Club of Hartford. |
| 1991 | Hill-Stead is designated a National Historic Landmark. |
| 2001 | Save America's Treasures names Hill-Stead an "official project." |
| 2003 | Hill-Stead is accredited by the American Association of Museums. |

# Further Reading

Brandegee, Arthur L. and Eddy H. Smith. *Farmington, Connecticut, The Village of Beautiful Homes*. Farmington, CT, 1906. Reprinted by the Farmington Historical Society, 1997.

Cunningham, Phyllis Fenn. *My Godmother, Theodate Pope Riddle*. Canaan, NH: published privately, 1983.

Emeny, Brooks. *Theodate Pope Riddle and the Founding of Avon Old Farms School*. Avon, CT: published privately, 1973 and 1977.

Hewitt, Mark A. *The Architect and the American Country House 1890-1940*. New Haven, CT: Yale University Press, 1990.

Katz, Sandra L. *Dearest of Geniuses, A Life of Theodate Pope Riddle*. Windsor, CT: Tide-Mark Press, 2003.

Mercer, William W., ed. *Avon Old Farms School*. Arlington, MA: Royalston Press, 2001.

Paine, Judith. *Theodate Pope Riddle: Her Life and Work*. Washington D.C: National Park Service, 1979.

Preston, Diana. *Lusitania, An Epic Tragedy*. New York, NY: Walker & Company, 2002.

Ramsey, Gordon, ed. *Aspiration and Perseverance, The History of Avon Old Farms School*. Avon, CT: Avon Old Farms School, 1984.

Smith, Sharon. *Theodate Pope Riddle, Her Life and Architecture*. Internet publication: www.valinet.com/~smithash/, 2002.

Stern, Robert A. M. *Pride of Place, Building the American Dream*. New York, NY: Houghton Mifflin, Co., 1988.

Torre, Susana, ed. *Women in American Architecture: A Historic and Contemporary Perspective, A Publication and Exhibition Organized by the Architectural League of New York*. New York, NY: Watson-Guptill Publications, 1977.